Thank You

FOR BEING MY

Teacher

Thank You

FOR BEING MY

Teacher

The quoted ideas expressed in this book (but not scripture verses) are not, in all cases, exact quotations, as some have been edited for clarity and brevity. In all cases, the author has attempted to maintain the speaker's original intent. In some cases, quoted material for this book was obtained from secondary sources, primarily print media. While every effort was made to ensure the accuracy of these sources, the accuracy cannot be guaranteed. For additions, deletions, corrections, or clarifications in future editions of this text, please contact Paul Shepherd, Executive Director for Elm Hill Books. Email pshepherd@elmhillbooks.com.

Scripture quotations are taken from:

The Holy Bible, King James Version (KJV)

The Holy Bible, New King James Version (NKJV) Copyright © 1982 by Thomas Nelson, Inc. Used by permission.

New Century Version (NCV) © 1987, 1988, 1991 by W Publishing, a division of Thomas Nelson, Inc. All rights reserved. Used by permission.

Cover Design by Denise Rosser
Page Layout by Bart Dawson

ISBN 1-4041-8456-2

Printed in the United States of America

To My Teacher

CONTENTS

INTRODUCTION

"Thank you for being my teacher!"—six words that have the power to warm the hearts and brighten the days of instructors everywhere. Because you're reading these words, it is likely *you* are a teacher. If so, congratulations! You have chosen one of the world's most important professions. You've committed yourself to the noble cause of molding impressionable minds. By doing so, you are reshaping our schools and our future. This text is intended as a way of saying thanks.

Henry Adams correctly observed, "A teacher affects eternity; he can never tell where his influence stops." Those words have never been truer than they are today. We live in a difficult, fast-paced, temptation-filled world. More than ever, our young people need the leadership of thoughtful mentors who are willing to teach by words and example, but not necessarily in that order.

So if you're fortunate to answer to the title of "teacher," whether in graduate school, high school, preschool, or Sunday school, rest assured your work does not go unnoticed by you students. To the contrary, when you touch the heart and mind of a single young person, you have, in a very real sense, refashioned eternity. Thank you, Teacher, for the memories and the mentoring. But not necessarily in that order.

Thank You for . . .
SHARING
YOUR KNOWLEDGE

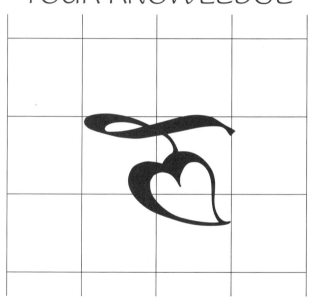

*It takes knowledge to fill a home
with rare and beautiful treasures.*

PROVERBS 24:4 NCV

Dear Teacher,

We have so much to learn—thank you for sharing your knowledge *and* your wisdom. You have helped us understand the value of education and the importance of lifetime learning. Sometimes, of course, we became tired of textbooks, tests, classrooms, and computer screens. But even when we would rather be *anyplace* other than school, you helped us focus on the things we needs to know. Because you were excited about learning, we became excited, too.

You have taught us education is the tool by which we come to know and appreciate the world in which we live. Thanks for that lesson—we will not forget it.

Signed,

Your Student

Knowledge is power.

—

FRANCIS BACON

Knowledge is the only instrument of production
that is not subject to diminishing returns.

J. M. CLARK

One good head is better
than a hundred strong hands.

THOMAS FULLER

An investment in knowledge
always pays the best interest.

BEN FRANKLIN

Nothing in the world is more dangerous
than sincere ignorance.

MARTIN LUTHER KING, JR.

Never stop acquiring specialized knowledge.

NAPOLEON HILL

It's what you know after you know it all
that counts.

HARRY S TRUMAN

We can easily forgive a child who is afraid
of the dark; the real tragedy of life is when
adults are afraid of the light.

PLATO

The empires of the future
are the empires of the mind.

WINSTON CHURCHILL

Wisdom is the power that enables us
to use knowledge.

THOMAS J. WATSON

Wonder rather than doubt
is the root of knowledge.
ABRAHAM JOSHUA HESCHEL

A man doesn't know what he knows
until he knows what he doesn't know.
LAURENCE J. PETER

It is better to know some of the questions
than to know all of the answers.
JAMES THURBER

The one exclusive sign of thorough knowledge is the ability to teach.

—

ARISTOTLE

Knowledge comes by eyes always open
and working hands, and there is no knowledge
that is not power.

JEREMY TAYLOR

Knowledge advances by steps and not by leaps.

LORD THOMAS BABINGTON MACAULAY

'Tis skill, not strength, that governs a ship.

THOMAS FULLER

The end of all knowledge should be
in virtuous action.

PHILLIP SIDNEY

Life is a festival only to the wise.

RALPH WALDO EMERSON

Wisdom is the supreme part of happiness.

SOPHOCLES

The wisest mind has something yet to learn.

GEORGE SANTAYANA

Thank You for . . .
YOUR ENTHUSIASM

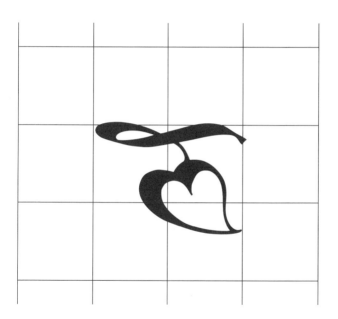

And whatever you do, do it heartily,
as to the Lord and not to men.

COLOSSIANS 3:23 NKJV

Dear Teacher,

Thank you for your enthusiasm. A teacher's attitude affects the mood of the entire classroom, and your enthusiasm is contagious. Because you are upbeat and enthusiastic, you make it easy to learn.

Mary Kay Ash once observed, "A mediocre idea that generates enthusiasm will go farther than a great idea that inspires no one." Because you have inspired us, we will carry *your* great ideas with us wherever we go.

Every production of genius must be the production of enthusiasm.

—

BENJAMIN DISRAELI

Every great accomplishment is
the story of a flaming heart.

ARNOLD H. GLASGOW

Sometimes success is due less to ability
than to zeal.

CHARLES BUXTON

Only passions, great passions,
can elevate the soul to great things

DENIS DIDEROT

When love and skill work together,
expect a masterpiece.

JOHN RUSKIN

We act as though comfort and luxury were
the chief requirements of life, when all we need
to make us really happy is something
to be enthusiastic about.

CHARLES KINGSLEY

A person can succeed at almost anything
for which he has unlimited enthusiasm.

CHARLES M. SCHWAB

Man's mind is not a container to be filled
but rather a fire to be kindled.

DOROTHEA BRANDE

Enthusiasm is nothing more or less than faith
in action.

HENRY CHESTER

Your enthusiasm will be infectious,
stimulating and attractive to others.
They will love your for it.
They will go for you and with you.

NORMAN VINCENT PEALE

Enthusiasm is everything.
It must be as taut and vibrating
as a guitar string.

PELÉ

Diligence applies to whatever you do.
Anything done in the Lord's service
is worth doing with enthusiasm and care.

JOHN MACARTHUR

There is very little
difference between
people, but that little
difference makes
a big difference.
That little difference
is attitude.

—

W. CLEMENT STONE

Success
is going from
failure to failure
without loss
of enthusiasm.

—

WINSTON CHURCHILL

Enthusiasm is one of the most powerful engines
of success. When you do a thing,
do it with your might. Put your whole soul
into it. Stamp it with your own personality.
Be active, be energetic, be enthusiastic
and faithful, and you will accomplish
your objective. Nothing great
was ever achieved without enthusiasm.

RALPH WALDO EMERSON

The key to unlocking the treasures in the art
of living, the secret of adding new dimensions
to your life, is simply this: Hold an adventurous
mental attitude. You cannot become bored
when you approach everything as an adventure!

WILFERD A. PETERSON

Wherever you are,
be all there.
Live to the hilt
every situation
you believe to be
the will of God.

—

JIM ELLIOT

Thank You for . . .
YOUR
ENCOURAGEMENT

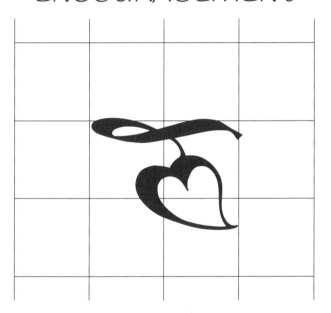

*But encourage each other every day
while it is "today." Help each other
so none of you will become hardened . . . .*

HEBREWS 3:13 NCV

Dear Teacher,

Thank you for your encouragement. Even when we did not believe in ourselves, you believed in us . . . and it showed.

Life is a team sport, and all of us need occasional pats on the back from our parents, our friends, and our teachers. As a thoughtful teacher, you know encouragement is a powerful tool for shaping the minds and hearts of your students. Thankfully, you never gave up on us, and you never stopped believing in our abilities. Because you believed, so, too, did we.

Creativity is
so delicate a flower
that praise tends to
make it bloom, while
discouragement
often nips it
in the bud.

—

ALEX F. OSBORN

Praise does wonders for our sense of hearing.
ARNOLD H. GLASGOW

Few things help an individual more than
to place responsibility upon him
and to let him know that you trust him.
BOOKER T. WASHINGTON

Encouragement is the oxygen of the soul.
JOHN MAXWELL

The true leader inspires in others self-trust,
guiding their eyes to the spirit of the goal.

BRONSON ALCOTT

Abilities wither under faultfinding,
blossom under encouragement.

DONALD A. LAIRD

Never tell a young person that anything
cannot be done. God may have been waiting
centuries for someone ignorant enough
of the impossible to do that very thing.

JOHN ANDREW HOLMES

The greatest good you can do for another
is not just to share your riches,
but to reveal to him his own.

BENJAMIN DISRAELI

Correction does much,
but encouragement does more.
Encouragement after censure
is as the sun after a shower.

GOETHE

Children have more need of models than critics.

JOSEPH JOUBERT

Greatness lies not in being strong,
but in the right use of strength,
and strength is not used rightly when it
only serves to carry a man above his fellows
for his own solitary glory. He is the greatest
whose strength carries up the most hearts
by the attraction of his own.

HENRY WARD BEECHER

It is the nature of man to rise to greatness
if greatness is expected of him.

JOHN STEINBECK

Kindness in words creates confidence.
Kindness in thinking creates wisdom.
Kindness in giving creates love.

LAO TZU

Great people are those who make others feel
that they, too, can become great.

MARK TWAIN

Invest in the human soul.
Who knows, it might be a diamond in the
rough.

MARY MCLEOD BETHUNE

Never miss an opportunity to say
a word of congratulations.

LYNDON BAINES JOHNSON

Trust men and they will trust you;
treat them greatly,
and they will show themselves great.

RALPH WALDO EMERSON

A lot of people
have gone further
than they thought
they could because
someone else
thought they could.

—

ZIG ZIGLAR

Criticism should not be querulous and wasting,
but instead it should be guiding,
instructive, and inspiring.

RALPH WALDO EMERSON

It does one good to hear applause.

WOOFGANG AMADEUS MOZART

To the loved, a word of affection is a morsel,
but to the love-starved,
a word of affection can be a feast.

MAX LUCADO

When someone does something good, applaud!
You'll make two people feel good.

SAM GOLDWYN

Thank You for . . .
YOUR KINDNESS

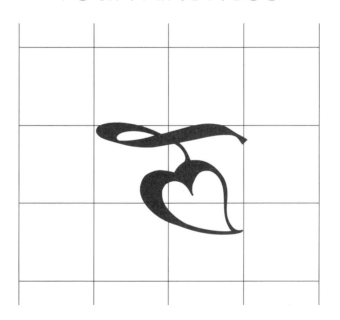

Pleasant words are like a honeycomb,
making people happy and healthy.

PROVERBS 16:24 NCV

Dear Teacher,

Amid the stressful moments of your demanding days, you slowed down long enough to sow seeds of kindness. And we noticed.

You were generous with your time and your praise. You were quick to share a thoughtful word, a genuine smile, or a helping hand. Through your words and your deeds, you demonstrated the power of compassion. May God bless you always, as you have blessed us.

Kindness is the universal language that all people understand.

—

JAKE GAITHER

The nicest thing we can do for
our heavenly Father is to be kind
to one of His children.

ST. TERESA OF AVILA

The essence of all religions is love, compassion
and tolerance. Kindness is my true religion.
The clear proof of a person's love of God
is if that person genuinely shows love
to fellow human beings.

DALAI LAMA

No act of kindness, no matter how small,
is ever wasted.

AESOP

Kindness is a golden chain by which
society is bound together.

GOETHE

Goodness is the only investment that never fails.

HENRY DAVID THOREAU

What wisdom can you find
that is greater than kindness?

JEAN-JACQUES ROSSEAU

You give little
when you give
your possessions.
It is when you give
of yourself
that you truly give.

—

KHALIL GIBRAN

Kind words do not cost much.
Although they cost little,
they accomplish much. Kind words produce
a beautiful image on men's souls.

PASCAL

Kind words can be short and easy to speak,
but their echoes are truly endless.

MOTHER TERESA

The older you get, the more you realize
that kindness is synonymous with happiness.

LIONEL BARRYMORE

Do everything in moderation
except when it comes to showing love
for your fellow man.

ROBERT GOULET

Wise sayings often fall on barren ground,
but a kind word is never thrown away.

SIR ARTHUR HELPS

The best portion of a good man's life is his little,
nameless, unremembered acts of kindness
and of love.

WILLIAM WORDSWORTH

Without kindness, there can be no true joy.

THOMAS CARLYLE

I shall pass through life but once.
Let me show kindness now,
as I shall not pass this way again.

WILLIAM PENN

Thank You for...
TEACHING ME
RESPONSIBILITY

*The one who plants and the one who waters
have the same purpose, and each will be
rewarded for his own work.*

1 CORINTHIANS 3:8 NCV

Dear Teacher,

Sometimes we behaved irresponsibly. When we did, you taught us the error of our ways. You taught us the greatest rewards in life are reserved for those of us who learn the art of self-discipline.

Doing the right thing is not always easy, especially when we're tired or frustrated. But doing the *wrong* thing almost always leads to trouble, and sometimes, it leads to BIG trouble.

You taught us that behaving responsibly may be harder in the beginning, but it's easier in the end. Thank you for the lesson. May we remember it always.

A sign of wisdom
and maturity is
when you come
to terms with the
realization that
your decisions cause
your rewards
and consequences.

—

DENIS WAITLEY

Action springs not from thought
but from a readiness for responsibility.
DIETRICH BONHOEFFER

The more you are willing to accept responsibility
for your actions, the more credibility
you will have.
BRIAN KOSLOW

No problem can be solved until an individual
assumes the responsibility for solving it.
M. SCOTT PECK

I believe that every right implies a responsibility;
every opportunity, an obligation;
every possession, a duty.

JOHN D. ROCKEFELLER, JR.

Only when we take full responsibility
for out actions can we shed the burdens
of our mistakes and go forward.

RICH DEVOS

The ability to accept responsibility
is the measure of the man.

ROY L. SMITH

Life ultimately
means taking
the responsibility
to find the right
answer to its
problems and
to fulfill the tasks
which it constantly
sets for the individual.

—

VIKTOR FRANKL

Transformation will begin in any life—in yours—
when you stand up and say:
"I'm responsible for the kind of person I am."

E. STANLEY JONES

The price of greatness is responsibility.

WINSTON CHURCHILL

Responsibility is the possibility of opportunity
culminating in inevitable fulfillment.

SRI CHINMOY

I learned early that if I wanted to achieve
anything in life, I'd have to do it myself.
I learned that I had to be accountable.

LENNY WILKINS

The willingness to accept responsibility
for one's own life is the source from which
self-respect springs.

JOAN DIDION

A nation is formed by the willingness
of each of us to share in the responsibility
for upholding the common good.

BARBARA JORDAN

Responsibility gravitates toward him
who gets ready for it, and power flows to him
and through him who can use it.

GEORGE WALTER FISKE

Thank Your for . . .
YOUR PATIENCE

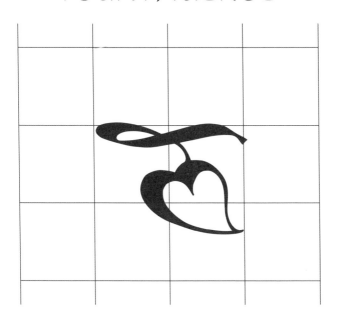

Patience is better than strength.

PROVERBS 16:32 NCV

Dear Teacher,

We know that teaching requires patience—*lots* of patience—because the classroom can be a frustrating place. But you never allowed the inevitable frustrations of life-here-at school to overwhelm you.

When we made a mess of things, you disciplined us, you forgave us, and you convinced us we could make amends.

You maintained your composure even when we didn't. When you demonstrated the power of patience, we watched, listened, and learned an important lesson. Thank you.

Genius is eternal patience.

MICHELANGELO

Patience is the companion of wisdom.

ST. AUGUSTINE

Patience and diligence, like faith,
move mountains.

WILLIAM PENN

We must learn to wait.
There is grace supplied to the one who waits.

MRS. CHARLES E. COWMAN

Time discovers truth.

SENECA

The strongest of all warriors are these two:
time and patience.

LEO TOLSTOY

All rising to a great place is by a winding stair.

FRANCIS BACON

There is no great achievement
that is not the result
of patient working and waiting.

JOSIAH GILBERT HOLLAND

Perseverance is
a great element
of success.
If you only knock
long enough
and loud enough
at the gate,
you are sure to
wake up somebody.
—

HENRY WADSWORTH LONGFELLOW

The greatest and most sublime power
is often simple patience.

HORACE BUSHNELL

Patience achieves more than force.

EDMUND BURKE

Have patience with all things,
but mostly with yourself. Don't lose courage
considering your own imperfections,
but instantly begin remedying them.
Every day begin the task anew.

ST. FRANCIS DE SALES

Endurance is nobler than strength,
and patience nobler than beauty.

JOHN RUSKIN

All things pass. Patience attains all it strives for.

ST. TERESA OF AVILA

Nothing great was ever done without much enduring.

—

CATHERINE OF SIENA

Thank You for . . .

YOUR EXAMPLE

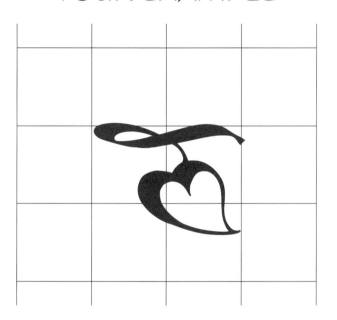

*In every way be an example of
doing good deeds. When you teach,
do it with honesty and seriousness.*

TITUS 2:7 NCV

Dear Teacher,

All of us need positive role models—thanks for being one. You have taught us some of life's most important lessons, not only by your words, but also by your actions.

You weren't always perfect—nobody is—but when you did made mistakes, you corrected them, moved on, and we learned.

Because of the example you've set, you are a powerful force for good inside the classroom and beyond . . . *far* beyond.

Example is not the main thing in influencing others — it is the only thing.

ALBERT SCHWEITZER

More depends upon my walk than upon my talk.

D. L. MOODY

Example is the school of humankind,
and they will learn at no other.

EDMUND BURKE

Example is a lesson that all can read.

GILBERT WEST

Nothing is so potent as the silent influence
of a good example.

JAMES KENT

A person who lives right, and is right,
has more power in his silence
than another has by words.

PHILLIPS BROOKS

Don't say things. What you are stands over you
all the while and thunders so loudly
that I cannot hear what you say to the contrary.

RALPH WALDO EMERSON

Live so as to explain thy doctrine by thy life.

MATTHEW PRIOR

You cannot not model. It's impossible.
People will see your example,
positive or negative,
as a pattern for the way life is lived.

STEPHEN COVEY

One example is worth a thousand arguments.

THOMAS CARLYLE

Nothing speaks louder or more powerfully
than a life of integrity.

CHARLES SWINDOLL

Leadership comes from competence.
Leadership is by example, not by talk.

BILL WALSH

He or she
is greatest who
contributes
the greatest
original practical
example.

WALT WHITMAN

Thank You for . . .
LISTENING

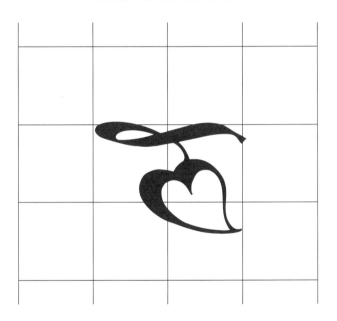

My dear brothers and sisters,
always be willing to listen and slow to speak.

JAMES 1:19 NCV

Dear Teacher,

Thanks for listening and for trying your best to understand. Sometimes you must have been frustrated by the things we said and did. But you listened anyway. Sometimes you understood us far better than we understood ourselves.

You were willing to share your advice which, regretfully, we often ignored. But you were also willing to let us make our own mistakes without saying, "I told you so."

Even when our words must have seemed silly or repetitive, you kept listening. That made all the difference.

The first duty of love is to listen.

—

PAUL TILLICH

It takes a great person to make a good listener.

ARTHUR HELPS

People will feel safer around you
and speak truthfully to you when
they feel you are listening intently to them.

BRIAN KOSLOW

One of the best ways to persuade others
is with your ears—by listening to them.

DEAN RUSK

Real unselfishness consists in sharing
the interests of others.

GEORGE SANTAYANA

There is no such thing as
a worthless conversation,
provided you know what to listen for.

JAMES NATHAN MILLER

Listen with sincerity.

JOE GIRARD

Listening is
a commitment and
a compliment.
It is a commitment
to understand how
the other person feels,
and it is a compliment
because it says,
"I care about what's
happening to you."

MATTHEW MCKAY

Listening, not imitation,
is the sincerest form of flattery.

JOYCE BROTHERS

The reason that we have two ears
and only one mouth is that we may listen
the more and talk the less.

ZENO OF CITIUM

Listening is its own reward;
there are no prizes to be won
except the pleasure of recognizing beauty
when one comes to it.

AARON COPLAND

If you want to be listened to,
you should put in time listening.

MARGE PIERCY

All wise people
share one trait
in common:
the ability
to listen.

—

FRANK TYGER

Thank You for ...

HELPING ME DREAM

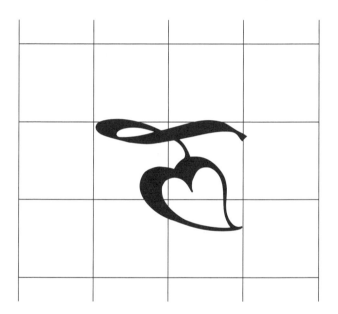

*But I will always have hope
and will praise you more and more.*

PSALMS 71:14 NCV

Dear Teacher,

Thanks for helping us dream. When we summoned the courage to confide in you, you supported us and encouraged us. If you harbored any doubts, you hid them.

Your faith has encouraged us to expect big things from life *and* from ourselves. Now it's up to each of us to transform our dreams into reality. Because of you, and others like you, we will keep believing in the power of our dreams. We will keep working until we make those dreams come true.

Our dreams are who we are.

—

BARBARA SHER

It is never too late to dream
or to start something new.

LUCI SWINDOLL

Nothing happens unless first a dream.

CARL SANDBURG

Whatever you can do,
or dream you can, begin it.
Boldness has genius, power, and magic in it.

GOETHE

If one advances confidently in the direction
of his dreams and endeavors to love the life
which he has imagined, he will meet with
a success unexpected in common hours.

HENRY DAVID THOREAU

When you reach for the stars,
you may not quite reach them,
but you won't come up
with a handful of mud, either.

LEO BURNETT

One's greatest asset is the capacity to dream.

MERV GRIFFIN

Twenty years from now you will be
more disappointed by the things you didn't do
than by he ones you did do. So throw off
the bowlines. Sail away from the safe harbor.
Catch the trade winds in your sails.
Explore. Dream. Discover.

MARK TWAIN

What a man can imagine he may
one day achieve.

NANCY HALE

It may be
those who
do most,
dream most.

—

STEPHEN LEACOCK

Man's reach should exceed his grasp,
or what's a heaven for?

ROBERT BROWNING

Dreams are ...
illustrations from the book your soul is writing.

MARSHA NORMAN

All men dream, but not equally.
Those who dream by night in the dusty recesses
of their minds wake in the day to find that
it was vanity; but the dreamers of the day
are dangerous men, for they may act their dream
with open eyes to make it possible.

THOMAS E. LAWRENCE

I have spread my dreams under your feet;
tread softly because you tread on my dreams.

WILLIAM BUTLER YEATS

If you can dream it, you can do it.

WALT DISNEY

Think big. Act big. Dream big.

CONRAD HILTON

They build too low who build beneath the skies.

EDWARD YOUNG

Everything is created twice—
first mentally, then physically.

GREG ANDERSON

Everything is in the mind.
Knowing what you want
is the first step in getting it.

MAE WEST

In the long run we only hit what we aim at.
Aim high.

HENRY DAVID THOREAU

Dreams do come true,
if we only wish
hard enough.
You can have anything
in life if you will sacrifice
everything else for it.
"What will you have?"
says God?
"Pay for it and take it."

—

JAMES BARRIE

Thank You for ...

DISCIPLINING ME

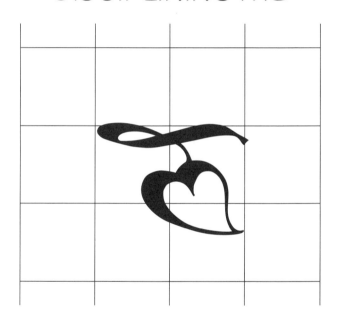

*Whoever accepts correction is on the way to life,
but whoever ignores correction
will lead others away from life.*

PROVERBS 10:17 NCV

Dear Teacher,

You are charged with a thankless task: controlling students who would prefer not to be controlled. Despite our wishes to the contrary, we need to be disciplined, and when we needed discipline, you provided it.

You have taught us that orderly behavior is a prerequisite for success both inside and outside the classroom. Thank you. As we grow up, all of us learn powerful, life-changing lessons about the rewards of self-discipline. Most of are still learning. You are helping.

Disciplinary problems become opportunities for conveying values, providing insights, and strengthening self-esteem.

—

HAIM GINOTT

Perhaps the most valuable result of all education
is the ability to make yourself do the thing
you have to do when it has to be done,
whether you like it or not.

ALDOUS HUXLEY

He who has never learned to obey cannot be
a good commander.

ARISTOTLE

Discipline without freedom is tyranny.
Freedom without discipline is chaos.

CULLEN HIGHTOWER

The goal of disciplining our children is
to encourage their growth as respectful,
responsible, self-disciplined individuals.

DON H. HIGHLANDER

Talking in class disturbs the teacher
and the class. The habit of self-control is not
easily acquired, but when the pupil has
his tongue under control, as, St. James says,
"He is able to bridle the whole body."

FANNY JACKSON COPPIN

Self-control is the quality that distinguishes
the fittest to survive.

GEORGE BERNARD SHAW

You cannot be disciplined in great things
and undisciplined in small things.

GEORGE S. PATTON

Obedience is the gateway through which knowledge, yes, and love, too, enter the mind of a child.

—

ANNIE SULLIVAN

No stream or river ever drives anything
until it is confined. No Niagara is ever turned
into light and power until it is harnessed.
No life ever grows until it is focused,
dedicated, disciplined.

HARRY EMERSON FOSDICK

Man cannot live without self-control.

ISAAC BASHEVIS SINGER

Discipline is the basic set of tools
we require to solve life's problems.

M. SCOTT PECK

Success isn't measured by money
or power or social rank.
Success is measured by your discipline
and inner peace.

MIKE DITKA

Loving a child doesn't mean giving in
to all his whims; to love him is to
bring out the best in him,
to teach him to love what is difficult.

NADIA BOULANGER

The alternative to discipline is disaster.

VANCE HAVNER

In reading the lives
of great people,
I found that the first
victory they won
was over themselves:
with all of them,
self-discipline
came first.

—

HARRY S TRUMAN

To be disciplined from within,
where all is permissible,
where all is concealed—that is the point.

MONTAIGNE

Self-discipline is an individual's greatest asset.

LOU HOLTZ

True will power and courage are not on
the battlefield, but in everyday conquests
over our inertia, laziness, and boredom.

D. L. MOODY

Thank You for . . .
INSPIRING
EXCELLENCE

Whatever work you do, do your best,
because you are going to the grave,
where there is no working . . . .

ECCLESIASTES 9:10 NCV

Dear Teacher,

Thank you for setting high standards. Had you not done so, we would have suffered. If little had been required of us, we would have responded with minimum effort. But because you demanded more, we gave more. We learned as much from our hard work as we did from the textbooks we studied.

You taught us excellence requires effort. Because you were willing to teach that lesson, we were compelled to learn it.

When it becomes
necessary
to do a thing,
the whole heart
and soul should
go into the measure,
or not attempt it.

—

THOMAS PAINE

Excellence is not an act but a habit.
The things you do the most are
the things you do the best.

MARVA COLLINS

With regard to excellence,
it is not enough to know,
but we must also try to put
that knowledge to use.

ARISTOTLE

People who consistently do things well
set their own standards
and make themselves measure up.

DENIS WAITLEY

Whatever is worth doing at all
is worth doing well.

LORD CHESTERFIELD

Give the world the best you have,
and the best will come back to you.

MADELINE BRIDGES

The secret of joy in work is contained in
one word: excellence.
To know how to do something well
is to enjoy it.

PEARL BUCK

Only a mediocre person is always at his best.

SOMERSET MAUGHAM

The best preparation for tomorrow is to do today's work superbly well.

—

WILLIAM OSLER

The great law of culture: Let each become
all that he was created capable of being.

THOMAS CARLYLE

There is a canyon of difference between
doing your best to glorify God
and doing whatever it takes to glorify yourself.
The quest for excellence is a mark of maturity.
The quest for power is childish.

MAX LUCADO

If you want to achieve excellence,
you can get there today.
As of this moment,
quit doing less-than-excellent work.

THOMAS J. WATSON

The quality of a person's life is
in direct proportion to his commitment
to excellence, regardless
of his chosen field of endeavor.

VINCE LOMBARDI

Doing the best at this moment puts you
in the best place for the next moment.

OPRAH WINFREY

Always dream and shoot higher
than you know you can do.
Don't bother just to be better
than your contemporaries or predecessors.
Try to be better than yourself.

WILLIAM FAULKNER

Thank You for . . .

YOUR OPTIMISM

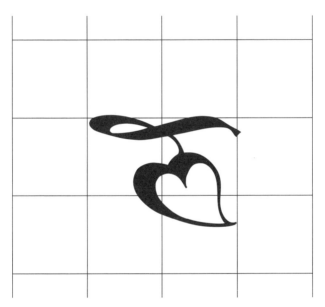

Finally, brethren, whatever things are true, whatever things are noble, whatever things are just, whatever things are pure, whatever things are lovely, whatever things are of good report, if there is any virtue and if there is anything praiseworthy—meditate on these things.

PHILIPPIANS 4:8 NKJV

Dear Teacher,

Thanks for sharing your optimistic spirit. You helped us believe in our hopes instead of our fears. When we fretted over the inevitable struggles of everyday living, you helped us regain perspective. When we worried about the uncertainty of tomorrow, you helped us focus on the opportunities of today.

Sometimes, of course, we will still fall prey to worry, frustration, anxiety, or sheer exhaustion. When we face life's inevitable challenges and disappointments, we will remember mentors like you, and we'll respond with courage, optimism, and perseverance.

Write it on
your heart that
every day is
the best day
of the year.

—

RALPH WALDO EMERSON

Act as if it were impossible to fail.

DOROTHEA BRANDE

Happiness is not a matter of events;
it depends on the tides of the mind.

ALICE MEYNELL

I feel an earnest and humble desire,
and shall do till I die, to increase
the stock of harmless cheerfulness.

CHARLES DICKENS

Think positively and masterfully,
with confidence and faith, and life becomes
more secure, more fraught with action,
richer in achievement and experience.

EDDIE RICKENBACKER

There is wisdom in the habit of looking at
the bright side of life.

FATHER FLANAGAN

We can accomplish almost anything
within our ability if we but think we can.

GEORGE MATTHEW ADAMS

A pessimist is one who makes difficulties
of his opportunities; an optimist is one
who makes opportunities of his difficulties.

HARRY S TRUMAN

No pessimist ever
discovered
the secrets of
the stars or sailed to
an uncharted land,
or opened
a new heaven to
the human spirit.

—

HELEN KELLER

The world of achievement has always
belonged to the optimist.

J. HAROLD WILKENS

To travel hopefully is better than to arrive.

JAMES JEANS

If you think you can, you can.
And if you think you can't, you're right.

MARY KAY ASH

The sun shines not on us, but in us.

JOHN MUIR

I have become my own version of an optimist.
If I can't make it through one door,
I'll go through another door—or I'll make
a door. Something terrific will come
no matter how dark the present.

JOAN RIVERS

An optimistic mind is a healthy mind.

LORETTA YOUNG

Be hopeful!
For tomorrow has never happened before.

ROBERT SCHULLER

The joy of
the mind is
the measure
of its strength.

—

NINON DE LENCLOS

I am an optimist. It does not seem
to be much use being anything else.

WINSTON CHURCHILL

The people whom I have seen succeed best
in life have always been cheerful
and hopeful people who went about their
business with a smile on their faces.

CHARLES KINGSLEY

Change your thoughts,
and you change your world.

NORMAN VINCENT PEALE

Thank You for . . .
SHARING
YOUR COURAGE

Be strong and of good courage, and do it;
do not fear nor be dismayed, for the Lord God—
my God—will be with you. He will not leave you
nor forsake you, until you have finished all
the work for the service of the house of the Lord.

1 CHRONICLES 28:20 NKJV

Dear Teacher,

I n difficult times, we learn lessons we could have learned in no other way: We learn about life, but more importantly, we learn about ourselves. Thank you for teaching us to live courageously.

Every human life, like every teaching career, is a tapestry of events: some grand, some not-so-grand, and some downright disappointing. You showed us that our disappointments and failures should never be considered "final" if we possess the courage to face our mistakes, and the wisdom to learn from them.

True courage is not
the brutal force
of vulgar heroes,
but the firm resolve
of virtue and reason.

—

ALFRED NORTH WHITEHEAD

God grant me the courage not to give up
fighting for what I think is right,
even if I think it is hopeless.

CHESTER NIMITZ

It takes courage to lead a life.
Any life.

ERICA JONG

Courage is not the absence of fear,
but rather the judgment that something else
is more important than fear.

AMBROSE REDMOON

Courage is contagious.

BILLY GRAHAM

Never forget that life can only be nobly inspired
and rightly lived if you take it bravely and
gallantly, as a splendid adventure in which
you are setting out into an unknown country,
to meet many a joy, to find many a comrade,
to win and lose many a battle.

ANNIE BESANT

Never let the fear of striking out get in your way.

BABE RUTH

Success is not measured by what a man
accomplishes, but by the opposition he has
encountered, and the courage with which
he maintained the struggle against
overwhelming odds.

CHARLES A. LINDBERGH, JR.

Courage is
the ladder
on which all other
virtues mount.

—

CLARE BOOTHE LUCE

Courage doesn't always roar.
Sometimes courage is that little voice at
the end of the day that says:
I'll try again tomorrow.

ANNE HUNNINGHAKE

Courage is grace under pressure.

ERNEST HEMINGWAY

When you get to the end of your rope,
tie a knot and hang on.

FRANKLIN D. ROOSEVELT

One isn't necessarily born with courage,
but one is born with potential.
Without courage, we cannot practice
any other virtue with consistency.
We can't be kind, true, merciful,
generous, or honest.

MAYA ANGELOU

To do anything in this world worth doing,
we must not stand back shivering
and thinking of the cold and danger,
but jump in, and scramble through
as well as we can.

SYDNEY SMITH

If I had permitted my failures to discourage me,
I cannot see any way in which
I would ever have made progress.

CALVIN COOLIDGE

We can do anything we want to do
if we stick to it long enough.

HELEN KELLER

Thank You for . . .

YOUR FAITH

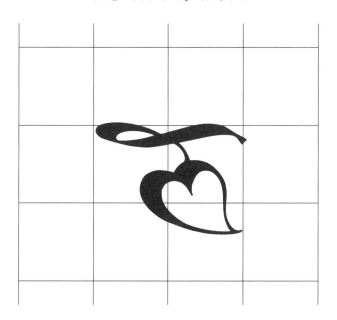

Now faith is the substance of things hoped for,
the evidence of things not seen.

HEBREWS 11:1 NKJV

Dear Teacher,

Life demands faith and lots of it. But sometimes, faith is in short supply, especially when we encounter circumstances that leave us discouraged or afraid. As youthful citizens living in a difficult age, we need faith in the future, faith in ourselves, and faith in our Creator.

All of us must suffer through times of disappointment and doubt. When our own faith waned, you willingly shared yours. For that, we will be forever grateful.

Faith is a spiritual spotlight that illuminates the path.

HELEN KELLER

Faith is the key that fits the door of hope.

ELAINE EMANS

Faith is not believing that God can,
but that God will!

ABRAHAM LINCOLN

Faith sees the invisible,
believes the unbelievable,
and receives the impossible.

CORRIE TEN BOOM

Faith is not belief without proof,
but trust without reservation.

ELTON TRUEBLOOD

Faith is like an empty, open hand stretched out
towards God, with nothing to offer
and everything to receive.

JOHN CALVIN

No one can give faith unless he has faith.
It is the persuaded who persuade.

JOSEPH JOURBERT

Faith can put a candle in the darkest night.

MARGARET SANGSTER

Without faith nothing is possible.
With it, nothing is impossible.

MARY MCLEOD BETHUNE

Nothing in life is more wonderful than faith.
It is the one great moving force
which we can neither weigh in
the balance or test in the crucible.

WILLIAM OSLER.

Faith never knows where it is being led,
but it loves the One who is leading.

OSWALD CHAMBERS

Christian faith is
a grand cathedral, with
divinely pictured windows.
Standing without,
you see no glory,
nor can imagine any.
But standing within,
every ray of light reveals
a harmony of
unspeakable splendors.

—

NATHANIEL HAWTHORNE

Faith leads us beyond ourselves.

POPE JOHN PAUL II

For we walk by faith, not by sight.

2 CORINTHIANS 5:7 NKJV

Trust in God. Even if you fail Him,
He will never fail you.

MARIE T. FREEMAN

Thank You for . . .
YOUR PRAYERS

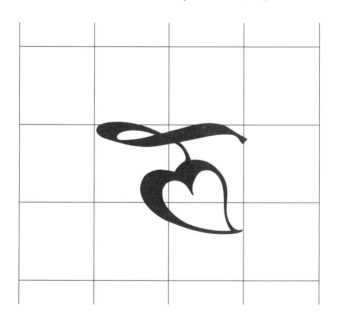

Be anxious for nothing, but in everything
by prayer and supplication, with thanksgiving,
let your requests be made known to God.

PHILIPPIANS 4:6 NKJV

Dear Teacher,

If you said any prayers on our behalf, you did so for a very good reason: you knew how badly we needed them! God certainly heard your prayers, and we have been blessed by them.

In today's uncertain world, all prayers are welcomed. Thank you for yours.

He who kneels most stands best.

—

D. L. MOODY

I have been driven many times to my knees
by the overwhelming conviction that
I had nowhere else to go. My own wisdom,
and that of all about me,
seemed insufficient for the day.

ABRAHAM LINCOLN

No man is greater than his prayer life.

LEONARD RAVENHILL

Prayer is that whole process that reminds us
of who God is and who we are.

MAX LUCADO

When you affirm big, believe big, and pray big, big things happen.

NORMAN VINCENT PEALE

God shapes the world by prayer.
The more praying there is in the world,
the better the world will be,
and the mightier will be the forces against evil.

E. M. BOUNDS

Prayer does not fit us for the greater work;
prayer is the greater work.

OSWALD CHAMBERS

God does amazing works through prayers
that seek to extend His grace to others.

SHIRLEY DOBSON

You pay God a compliment
by asking great things of Him.

ST. TERESA OF AVILA

If you lack knowledge, go to school.
If you lack wisdom, get on your knees.

VANCE HAVNER

God is always listening.

STORMIE OMARTIAN

What God gives in answer to our prayers
will always be the thing we most urgently need,
and it will always be sufficient.

ELISABETH ELLIOT

The key to a blessed life is to have
a listening heart that longs to know
what the Lord is saying.

JIM CYMBALA

Do not pray for easy lives.
Pray to be stronger men.

JOHN F. KENNEDY

Prayer may not change things for you,
but it for sure changes you for things.

SAMUEL M. SHOEMAKER

When we pray, we have linked ourselves
with Divine purposes, and we therefore have
Divine power at our disposal for human living.

E. STANLEY JONES

The purpose of all prayer is to find God's will
and to make that will our prayer.

CATHERINE MARSHALL

The sovereign cure for worry is prayer.

WILLIAM JAMES

Indeed, wisdom and discernment are among
the natural results of a prayer-filled life.

RICHARD FOSTER

I have so much to do that I spend hours
in prayer before I am able to do it.

JOHN WESLEY

He that is never on his knees on earth,
shall never stand upon his feet in heaven.

C. H. SPURGEON

Prayer does not change God;
it changes me.

C. S. LEWIS

Prayer connects us
with God's limitless potential.

HENRY BLACKABY

Thank You for ...
BEING A TEACHER

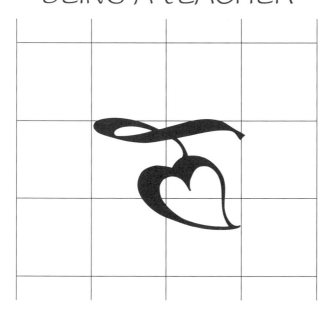

Be gentle to all, able to teach, patient.

2 TIMOTHY 2:24 NKJV

Dear Teacher,

Thank you. Thanks for being someone we can look up to and someone we can learn from. Thanks for teaching us lessons from textbooks and lessons about life. Thank you for your concern, your commitment, and your encouragement.

Thanks for making our classes interesting, even when *we were* not very interested. Thanks for maintaining order in the classroom, even when *we were* not particularly orderly. Thank you for the lessons you taught, the papers you graded, the homework you corrected, and the time you invested after class. We knew your job was demanding, and we appreciated your dedication.

Finally, thanks for doing your part to make this world a better place. When you became a teacher, you did so because you wanted to help others. You have succeeded. You have helped to shape our thoughts and direct our lives. Because of you, we have learned and grown. We will remember you always.

Signed,

Your Students

I touch the future. I teach.

—

CHRISTA MCAUILFFE

It is better to light one small candle
than to curse the darkness.

CONFUCIUS

A good teacher is one who helps you become
who you feel yourself to be.
A good teacher is also one who says
something you won't understand
until ten years later.

JULIUS LESTER

In the washroom, we need a soap dispenser.
In the classroom, we need a hope dispenser.

MARIE T. FREEMAN

What could be more important than equipping
the next generation with the character
and competence they need
to become successful.

COLIN POWELL

What greater work is there than training
the mind and forming the habits of the young?

ST. JOHN CHRYSOSTOM

Good teaching is one-fourth preparation
and three-fourths pure theatre.

GAIL GODWIN

A teacher affects eternity; he can never tell where his influence stops.

—

HENRY ADAMS

Let it be lost on no one that one
of the most important jobs in this country
is teaching. Teachers can influence
and motivate an entire generation.

ABIGAIL VAN BUREN

Most of us end up with no more than five
or six people who remember us.
Teachers have thousands of people who
remember them for the rest of their lives.

ANDY ROONEY

The dream begins, most of the time,
with a teacher who believes in you,
who tugs and pushes and leads you on
to the next plateau, sometimes poking you
with a sharp stick called truth.

DAN RATHER

Blessed is the influence of one true,
loving human being upon another.

GEORGE ELIOT

In a completely rational society,
the best of us would aspire to be teachers
and the rest of us would have to settle for
something less, because passing civilization
along from one generation to the next ought
to be the highest honor and the highest
responsibility anyone could have.

LEE IACOCCA

The mediocre teacher tells.
The good teacher explains.
The superior teacher demonstrates.
The great teacher inspires.

WILLIAM WARD

It is the supreme art of the teacher to awaken
joy in creative expression and knowledge.

ALBERT EINSTEIN

To believe in a child is to believe in
the future. Through their aspirations
they will save the world. With their
combined knowledge the turbulent
seas of hate and injustice will be
calmed. They will champion
the causes of life's underdogs, forging
a society without class discrimination.
They will supply humanity with music
and beauty as it has never known.
They will endure. Towards these ends
I pledge my life's work. I will supply
the children with tools and knowledge
to overcome the obstacles.
I will pass on the wisdom of my years
and temper it with patience.
I shall impact in each child the desire
to fulfill his or her dream. I shall teach.

—

HENRY JAMES

Better than a thousand days of diligent study
is one day with a great teacher.

JAPANESE PROVERB

Teachers are those who use themselves
as bridges, over which they invite their students
to cross; then having facilitated their crossing,
joyfully collapse, encouraging them
to create bridges of their own.

NIKOS KAZANTZAKIS

A master can tell you what he expects
of you. A teacher, though,
awakens your own expectations.

PATRICIA NEAL

Nine-tenths of education is encouragement.

ANATOLE FRANCE

The essence of teaching is to make
learning contagious,
to have one idea spark another.

MARVA COLLINS

Teaching is not the filling of the pail,
but the lighting of the fire.

WILLIAM BUTLER YEATS

If we work in marble,
it will perish;
if we work upon brass,
time will efface it;
if we rear temples, they
will crumble into dust;
but if we work upon
immortal minds and instill
in them just principles,
we are then engraving upon
tablets which no time will
efface, but will brighten
and brighten to all eternity.

—

DANIEL WEBSTER

About Criswell Freeman

Criswell Freeman's books have sold millions of copies, yet his name is largely unknown to the general public. *The Wall Street Journal* observed, "Normally, a tally like that would put a writer on the bestseller lists. But Freeman is hardly a household name." And that's exactly how the author likes it.

The Washington Post called Freeman "possibly the most prolific 'quote book' writer in America." With little fanfare, Dr. Freeman has compiled and edited well over a hundred titles that have now sold over 8,000,000 copies.

Freeman began his writing career as a self-help author (his first book was entitled *When Life Throws You a Curveball, Hit It*). Today, Freeman's writings focus on the Good News of God's Holy Word. Criswell is a Doctor of Clinical Psychology (he earned his degree from the Adler School of Professional Psychology in Chicago). He earned his undergraduate degree at Vanderbilt University. Freeman also attended classes at The Southern Baptist Theological Seminary in Louisville where he studied under the noted pastoral counselor Wayne Oates.

Criswell lives in Nashville, Tennessee. He is married and has two daughters.